STUDY GUIDE

GENESIS

Authentic
LIFESTYLE

First published in 2003 by Authentic Lifestyle

09 08 07 06 05 04 03   7 6 5 4 3 2 1

Authentic Lifestyle is an imprint of Authentic Media,
P.O. Box 300, Carlisle, Cumbria, CA3 0QS, UK
and P.O. Box 1047, Waynesboro, GA 30830-2047, USA

www.paternoster-publishing.com

British Library Cataloguing in Publication Data
A catalogue record for this book is available from the British Library

ISBN 1-85078-503-1

Cover Design by Gallison Design
Typeset by WestKey Ltd, Falmouth, Cornwall
Printed in the U.S.A.

For Liz,
my wonderful wife
and my best friend

Contents

1. The Beginning of the Cosmos   1

2. The Beginning of Humanity   7

3. The Beginning of Sin and Death   13

4. The Beginning of Judgement   21

5. The Beginning of the Church   27

6. The Beginning of the Sacraments   33

7. The Beginning of Election   41

8. The Beginning of Israel   47

9. The Beginning of Exile   53

10. The End of the Beginning   59

The Book of Genesis

The Book of Genesis is the book of beginnings. It sets the scene for everything in the whole Bible. In this book we learn about the creation of everything, the visible and the invisible. We discover how the universe was created. Genesis also teaches us where evil came from, explains the presence of pain, suffering and death in the world, and clearly reveals the solutions to these problems.

1. The Beginning of the Cosmos

Chapter 1

Key Truth: The whole creation was made by God the Father, through God the Son, by God the Holy Spirit.

1. The Work of Creation was a Trinitarian Work

The Bible begins with 'God'. There is no introduction or proof. We are simply told that 'God' created everything. The word used for 'God' here is the Hebrew word 'Elohim'. What is so striking about this word is that it is a plural. The God who we meet in Genesis chapter 1 is not a lonely god. There is only One God, but that One God is not just one person. He is a unity of Three Persons – and we see them all at work in these opening verses. We see the Spirit of God hovering over the water in verse 2, waiting for the Word of God to give direction and focus. Then, in verse 3, God speaks His Word.

When a person first reads this they might not think anything of it – but when we see how John explains this chapter of Genesis at the beginning of his gospel (John chapter 1), we are ready to read it more carefully. In the book of Genesis we are going to meet a Divine Person who has the title 'The Word of God'. We will discover that this Word of God is the central figure, not only in the book of Genesis, but in the whole Bible. We will see that every work of God in the Bible is from the Father, through the Son and by the Holy Spirit.

2. The Work of Creation was Unopposed

Through the Word of God the whole universe came into existence. There was nothing at all before that.

This is very important, because God did not have to work with material that was already there. Everything was made from scratch just as He wanted it to be. Everything was designed to be just what God the Father wanted, and His Son, the Word, executed His designs by the power of the Spirit. There was no opposition at all.

Ancient myths speak of the universe being formed by a war between the gods and modern myths speak of order randomly arising out of chaos – but all these stories are just empty myths. The Bible explains that everything was created without any conflict or compromise.

3. The Work of Creation Took Six Days

The work of creation was not an endlessly long work in progress. The Bible tells us it was all done in six days, showing the absolute power and wisdom of the Living God. The amazing way in which God brings such order and structure into everything gives us such confidence in the creation. The animals and plants are not random collections of genes, but works of art.

Notice how the first three days stand in parallel to the second three days.

Day 1 – Light	Day 4 – The lights
Day 2 – The water and the air	Day 5 – The animals of the water and the air.
Day 3 – The dry land	Day 6 – The animals of the dry land.

There have been different views about whether these six days were real days. Some have spoken of them as symbolic of very long periods of time, and others have seen them as indicating six phases in a long history of evolution. However, we offer three reasons for understanding these days as ordinary 24-hour days:

1. The Bible is the best guide for the meaning of the Bible. The best way to know the meaning of one part of the Bible is when another part of the Bible tells us! In Exodus 20:8–11 the LORD God[1] refers back to Genesis chapter 1 and speaks of the days of creation as six ordinary days.

---

[1] We will normally use the word LORD in capitals to refer to the God of Israel, simply because that is the procedure followed in most English translations of the Bible, to refer to Yahweh.

2. Exodus 20 and Genesis 2:2–3 tell us that the way we organise our days into weeks is based on that very first week where God worked for six days and rested on the seventh. If God had worked with endless, unceasing labour for billions of years before entering into His rest, then His model of the Sabbath is very weak.
3. The word used for 'day' in the Genesis chapter 1 is the Hebrew word 'yom'. Although this word can have a range of meanings (covering daytime as opposed to night-time, a 24-hour period, a specific time, or even a whole year) when this word is used with a **number** in the Bible (a total of 410 times), it **always** refers to a regular 24-hour day. Furthermore, this word 'yom' is used 23 times outside of Genesis 1 along with the words 'evening' or 'morning', and in every occasion, it refers to an ordinary day.

4. The Work of Creation Was Very Good

All the bad things in the creation were not there in the beginning. In the beginning everything was good, free from any evil at all. The reason why the theory of evolution is opposed so vehemently by so many Christians is that the theory insists that death and suffering have always existed and are natural parts of the universe. A common view of science and theology is that they exist in totally different areas and do not have any common ground from which to speak to each other. It is said that theology deals with meaning and science deals with fact. However, the Bible does not separate facts and meaning in this way. It is not easy to see how we can keep our thinking about death in science completely separate from our thinking about death in the Bible.

Sometimes people speak as if anything physical or material is a bit suspicious or inferior. This is wrong, because when God made everything He called it **all** 'good'. The physical and the spiritual, the seen and the unseen, the earth and the heavens were all made together at the same time and both parts of the creation were judged to be 'very good'. In our study of Genesis chapter 3 we will discover where all the evil, pain and suffering have come from.

5. The Work of Creation Shows the Grace of God

The work of creation was a display of the overflowing grace and generosity of God. At the end of His six days of work, Adam and Eve were given a day of rest. It is a wonderful picture of the gospel. Before they do any work, they enter into His rest.

Genesis 1:2 is a curious verse. Why were the heavens and the earth 'formless and empty' for this brief time before the Word of God was presented in verse 3? Why would God create in such a way?

The same expression is used in Jeremiah 4:23. The prophet is given a terrible vision of a world in which not even the people of God know the Living God. In such a world Jeremiah sees that it has become 'formless and empty', devoid of life and light. Thus the meaning of Genesis 1:2 is clear. For a brief moment on the first morning of creation, before the Word of God is openly revealed, the universe stands in chaos and darkness. We are taught that without the Word of God there is nothing but barren, empty darkness. In the first chapter of John's Gospel these wonderful truths are brought out of Genesis chapter 1.

Further Questions:

1. The universe is not a random occurrence, but a masterpiece of design. What does this mean for genetic research and genetic modifications?
2. There are many modern theories about the origin of the universe and life on earth. How should the Bible relate to these theories?
3. So often, our relationship with God becomes over-familiar and casual. How can a chapter like this challenge that?
4. How can we use this chapter of Genesis in our evangelism?
5. Verse 5: Before the creation of the sun and the moon, God marks off the days as 'evening and morning'. Even the sun and the moon must later fit into the daily cycle that God has established. The Bible, especially the Psalms, take this daily cycle of evening and morning very seriously. The night is a time of testing, whereas the morning is the time of security (Psalm 77:2, 30:5). Why did God define the day from evening to morning, rather than from morning to evening?[2]

---

[2] Hint: in the Bible, the darkness is overcome by the light, not the light overcome by the darkness.

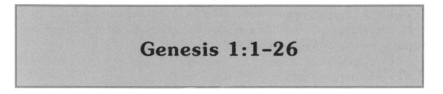

Genesis 1:1-26

Genesis chapter 1 sets the scene for all that happens in the rest of the Bible. This is why it has been taken so seriously and studied in such depth for thousands of years. We are shown the creation of all things visible and invisible, and in this way all the myths and superstitions of the world, both ancient and modern, are destroyed.

Verses 1-2: Look up Colossians 1:15-16. What is meant by 'the heavens and the earth'? When was the unseen creation (including the angels) created?

Verses 3-5: Why did God spend a whole day on the creation of light? Why was it so important to separate the light from the darkness? (John 3:19-21)

Verses 6-13: When He created, the Father wrote into creation important lessons about our relationship with Him. He spends an entire day on water which is used to teach us many things throughout the Bible. He spends a whole day producing the fruit-bearing plants. Can we think of some of the lessons that the Bible teaches through plants? (Psalm 1, John 12:24 and 1 Corinthians 15:35-49; Psalm 103:15)

Verses 14-19: So much seems to happen on the fourth day. Not only does God create the sun and the moon, but 'He also made the stars'. The creation of the whole of the rest of the universe is dealt with in one single phrase. Today, people tend to think of Earth as a minor planet at the edge of a minor galaxy. How does the work of the fourth day give us a true perspective on the universe?

Verses 20-26: What is the relationship between humanity and all the animals of the air, water and land?

Week of Readings

Sunday:	2 Peter 3
Monday:	Genesis 1:1–26
Tuesday:	Colossians 1:15–23
Wednesday:	Psalm 19
Thursday:	Job 38
Friday:	Psalm 104
Saturday:	Isaiah 11:1–9 (esp. 6–9)

2. The Beginning of Humanity

Chapter 2

Key Truth: The human race was created to imitate the way the Father and the Son love each other.

1. Humanity was Created as Male and Female

Although it sounds obvious, it is fundamental to realise that we were created as male and female. Being male and female is neither an accident of fate nor a lifestyle choice. It lies so much deeper in our original creation. Part of our most basic identity is found in our being male or female – both equally human.

Sexuality has become very complex in the absence of this basic framework. Many modern books on sexuality do not even make reference to the basic fact of our being male or female. This differentiation is not a hidden secret for us to discover about ourselves, but founded in our basic bodily form.

Far from being a repressive idea, this is a liberating truth. Even in our fallen and sinful struggles the basic facts of our creation as male and female provide an immovable anchor.

2. Humanity was Created in the Image of God

Following the story of the formation of Eve out of Adam is crucial for our understanding of humanity. Eve was not a separate creation, as if she was a different kind of creature. No, Adam was divided up, split into two. Eve is not different to Adam. She is the **alter ego**, the other self, of Adam. Both Adam and Eve can look back to their original unity.[1]

---

[1] Karl Barth makes the point that Adam's bride is produced through Adam's death-like sleep – just as the Church, Christ's bride, is produced through Christ's death on the Cross.

When we start from this truth we can understand the kind of language used about humanity being in the image of God. We are told that we were made in the image of God as we were created as male and female. Humanity is one, yet many – united and diverse. Adam and Eve are different persons, yet become one in their loving relationship to each other.

In marriage we see this basic pattern of unity in love very clearly, but it extends beyond marriage to the whole human family. We must never forget that there is only one human family. The whole population of the earth is the extended family of Adam and Eve, Acts 17:26. Adam and Eve became one flesh in their union, and out of that union came others who are also one flesh with Adam and Eve. Although it is hard to see humanity as one united family today, nevertheless that is God's vision.

From this we can see how the human race is in the image of God. The most basic truth about God is that He is a unity of Three Persons – Father, Son, and Holy Spirit. Sometimes people think of the image of God in very abstract ways – reason, language, imagination, spirituality. But animals and angels have all these things and are not described as in the 'image of God'.

3. Humanity was Created to Rule Over the World

It is easy to forget the way in which Adam was created. The LORD God did not simply command him to exist in the way that everything else had been created. Adam was formed from the clay, from the dust of the earth. Adam was hand-made by the LORD God. Can we imagine the LORD God bending down to mould the clay into this human form and then breathing into his nostrils?

Not only does this show us the loving intimacy that existed from the very beginning between God and humanity, but it also reminds us of the place of humanity within the universe. Sometimes people speak as if humanity was a temporary visitor on the planet earth, whereas our home is somewhere else in a spiritual place. This is not true. The Bible shows us as formed out of the very stuff of the universe. There is no other creature which is so tied to the physical material of the earth. Humanity is a spiritual, living, breathing bit of clay.

One part of the ground was formed up into a person, and out of that one clay-man the whole human race has grown. The name 'Adam' means 'earth-creature'.

This is why it is so right for humanity to have such great responsibility for the creation. We were formed to be the rulers of the world, under the ultimate rule of Christ. One songwriter refers to Adam and Eve as the King and Queen of creation.

If we wonder how it can be that the actions of humanity could have brought such catastrophe upon the whole universe or how it can be that the whole universe waits for the redemption of humanity (Romans 8:18–25), then we need to remember how God formed and appointed humanity at the beginning.

4. Humanity was Created without Sin, Shame or Death

'To err is human' – or so the saying goes. All our experience of human life around us confirms that. Every human we ever see is sinful and dies. We find it hard to imagine human life as anything other than a life of shame and mortality. The only people who know no shame are those who are shameless, too corrupt to even acknowledge their shame. Most of us know all about the things we have done, thought and felt that we do not want anyone to know about.

However, that is not how we were created. Adam and Eve knew no shame. They were naked. They had nothing to hide. They were comfortable with each other and the LORD God. They knew no sin.

Death was not part of the creation at the beginning. Adam and Eve could look forward to everlasting lives, free from all suffering, pain and death. They had no experience of what seems such a basic part of life today. Death was so alien to that original life that humanity and the animals were even given a vegetarian diet! (1:29–30).

It is vital that we keep hold of this truth. So many people throughout history have imagined that pain and suffering and death are simply natural parts of life in the universe. If that were so then the only way we could escape pain and death would be to escape from the universe itself. Nearly all the false views of the creation come from thinking of death as a natural part of life in the creation. However, we must daily remind ourselves that death and pain and suffering are intruders into God's very good creation.

We might find it hard to imagine what life must have been like before sin and death – or what it will be like after Jesus returns to renew it all – but we must not allow our current experience to determine our thinking and living.

Further Questions:

1. How does sexual sin affect our understanding of God?
2. It has been said that science fiction is the last area of culture in which real theology can be done. Perhaps this is so, but to what extent do science fiction scenarios which treat humanity as simply one of many races in the universe undermine the biblical view of humanity?
3. Some Christians have argued that all Christians should be vegetarians because of Genesis 1:29–30. This is a question that we should bear in mind as we go through the book of Genesis – but what is our response to this? Will there be any meat eating at all after the return of Jesus?

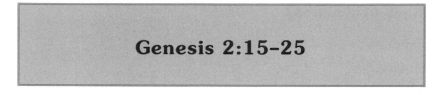

Genesis 2:15-25

This part of Genesis is referred to many times in the rest of the Bible. It forms a kind of manifesto for humanity.

Verses 15-17: Adam was not put in God's Garden as a mere spectator, but to work and care for it. Adam was told that he was free – but this freedom is guarded with one warning. Why did the LORD plant the tree of the knowledge of good and evil in the middle of the Garden? How is Adam's freedom defined here? How does Biblical freedom compare with the way that the world defines freedom? (Cf. John 8:31–36)

Verse 18: Everything in the creation was very good – except one thing. Adam being alone was 'not good'. Why?

Verses 19-20: In the Bible a name represents everything about a person. A person's name is their nature and character (Exodus 34:5–7). What does this tell us about Adam's activity in these verses?

Verses 21-22: 'Rib' is a bit weak. The Hebrew conveys more than that. It seems more like Adam being split into two, almost as if Adam and Eve were both formed out of the original Adam. What does this tell us about the relationship between man and woman?

Verses 23-24: Marriage is a divine invention. Sex was given before sin ever existed. According to the Bible, in marriage, man and woman become one flesh. What does this tell us about the meaning of sex? See 1 Corinthians 6:16.

Verse 25: What does this verse tell us about the human body? What should we make of Christian naturism?

Week of Readings

Sunday:	Ephesians 5:21–6:4
Monday:	Genesis 1:26–2:3
Tuesday:	Genesis 2:4–2:25
Wednesday:	Psalm 8
Thursday:	1 Corinthians 11:1–16
Friday:	John 17
Saturday:	Matthew 19:1–15

3. The Beginning of Sin and Death

Chapters 3-5

> **Key Truth:** The reason for all the evil and suffering in the universe is sin.

1. The Serpent

The serpent is introduced as a very suspicious character, as more 'crafty' than any of the wild animals. Does this mean that he was already sinful? The problem lies in the English translation. The Hebrew word is the word used throughout the book of Proverbs to indicate wisdom and cleverness. Perhaps the simple word 'clever' is best here – 'the serpent was the cleverest of the wild animals'.

Who is this serpent? That is easy to answer – it is Lucifer, who in Revelation 20:2 is referred to as 'the dragon, that ancient serpent, who is the devil or Satan'. There doesn't seem to be any reason to doubt that Moses knew what he was writing about.

But, what is Lucifer doing in the garden? Why didn't the LORD protect humanity from this terribly evil spirit?

Ezekiel 28 is an amazing chapter which tells us a lot about the origin of evil in Satan. The first part of Ezekiel chapter 28 (verses 1–10) is addressed to a man who thinks that he is a god, the ruler of Tyre. However, from verse 11 it is as if the Word of the LORD addresses a bigger, darker figure who stands behind the human ruler. This figure was the model of perfection in Eden, the garden of God. He was anointed as a guardian cherub and had free access to the holy mount of God. Verse 15 is striking: 'You were blameless in your ways from the day you were created till wickedness was found in you.' He was exiled to live on earth because of his pride. Isaiah 14 fills out this history, giving us his name, Lucifer (the morning star). In Isaiah 14:12–15 we learn that he decided that he could be like the Most High, like God.

If we put all this together we see that Lucifer was not evil when he was first in the Garden of Eden. There was no design fault in him, and at first he was blameless in Eden. However, just as we see in his conversation with Eve, when he recommends that Adam and Eve become like the Most High, he also had such plans himself. Everything said about Satan in Scripture fits the events of Genesis 3. We have no need to invent another history of an angelic war or a pre-creation spiritual rebellion.

2. The Woman

Eve has to face the serpent's deceit. Wasn't this a bit unfair? How could she outwit the cleverest of all creatures, the one who was the model of perfection and wisdom?

Eve had everything she needed. The LORD God had warned them not to eat from the tree of the knowledge of good and evil. What more did Eve need?

Nevertheless, she listened to Satan's reasoning. Was it at this time that Satan finally conceived his plan to be like the Most High? Jesus described him as a liar and a murder from the beginning (John 8:44) – presumably because his first acts of sin were lying to Eve and murdering the human race.

3. The Man

Adam was standing right next to Eve while she was being tempted (Genesis 3:6) – and he never said anything. He allowed her to be deceived and offered her no support, despite the fact that God had given Eve to Adam as a companion.

Adam needed no persuasion to eat the fruit. He simply took it and ate.

Straight away the corruption of sin took hold of their hearts and minds. God had created them naked – but now that they were ashamed of what they had done, they could no longer stand to be naked in each other's presence. They tried to cover up their shame with a few fig leaves.

This terrible first sin, when Adam and Eve failed to trust what the LORD had told them, has historically been called The Fall (although it is not a term found in the Bible).

4. The LORD God

As Adam and Eve vainly tried to hide their guilt, the LORD God came for an evening walk in His Garden. This tells us straight away that it was the

Second Person of the Trinity who had come to see them – as no-one has ever seen the Father at any time (John 1:18).

This was the One who had only ever given them good things. He had made them with His own hands and given them each other. He had never given them any reason to hide from Him or fear Him. Yet, the effect of their sin was so deep and rapid that they simply wanted to hide away from their loving LORD God.

When they crouch in the trees as He walks towards them, the LORD does not thunder in anger or drag them out into the open. He first gives them the chance to draw near to Him in repentance and faith – 'Adam, where are you?'

The LORD gives Adam an opportunity to confess his sin – but Adam simply decides to blame Eve, 'who YOU gave me'. Eve in turn blames Satan. The classic signs of the sinful heart are so clear so soon.

5. The Curse

The LORD does not give Satan the chance to explain himself. He can already see the long-running war that will exist between them. He directly curses Satan, exiling him to spend his existence on earth away from heaven.

It seems very bleak. Satan is imprisoned on earth, and it looks as if humanity would be left as soldiers in Satan's army. Yet, Genesis 3:15 is one of the great gospel verses of the Bible. Satan is not allowed to form an alliance with humanity. Rather, the LORD sets humanity and Satan against each other. How? By promising that a human child, born of woman, would destroy Satan, even though Satan would be able to wound the heel of this coming Redeemer. What a glorious promise! The first Gospel sermon is preached by Christ as He prophesies His own future birth!

Is it right to use the word 'Christ' in our study of the book of Genesis to identify the Promised One, the second Person of the Trinity? Some may feel that 'Christ' is a New Testament word which shouldn't be used in the Old Testament. This is, of course, quite mistaken. It is the Greek translation of the Hebrew word 'Messiah'. It is therefore an Old Testament term which is used in the New Testament. The New Testament is happy to use the word 'Christ' in its own studies of the Old Testament (see for example, 1 Corinthians 10:4). We should always follow the examples of Bible study set out for us in the Bible! So in Hebrews 11:26, the author uses the word 'Christ' to name the One who was the object of Moses' faith and hope. Therefore, it seems right when we are studying the writings of Moses to follow the example of Hebrews 11 and identify the promised Mediator with one of His most common titles. The 'Jews for Jesus' website is a treasure trove of biblical studies on these issues[1].

Some have said that we should not speak about Christ in the Old Testament because He is the mystery 'which was not made known to men in other generations as it has now been revealed' [Ephesians 3:5]. However, the next verse of Ephesians 3 explains that the mystery is not Christ, but the way in which Israel was extended out to include Gentiles all over the world – 'this mystery is that through the gospel the Gentiles are heirs **together** with Israel, members **together** of one body, and sharers **together** in the promise in' Jesus the Messiah. We see the same explanation of this 'mystery' in Romans 16:26 where the truth about the Messiah in the prophetic writings is now being revealed to the whole world.

Eve must face judgement next. By her child-bearing, sin and Satan would be destroyed, and it is in her child-bearing that the curse of sin is felt. Furthermore, her relationship with her husband is also spoiled, becoming a battle of the sexes, rather than the wonderful unity modelled on God that they were created to enjoy (1 Corinthians 11:3).

The judgement against Adam is the most severe. Because of Adam the whole of creation is cursed, subject to a frustrating curse of death and decay (Romans 8:18–25). The ground would produce nothing but thorns and thistles unless farmed through hard work and sweat to produce food. Created for everlasting immortal life, Adam drags the human race down into the grave.

At the end of chapter 3 we see another great gospel sign. Adam and Eve had tried to cover up their sin through their own efforts with fig leaves. The LORD God shows them what is required to cover up sin – the shed blood of sacrifice. He kills a couple of animals to provide animal skin coverings for them. How shocking it must have been for Adam and Eve to see for the first time what death looks like!

In chapter 4:1 Eve is mistaken when she thinks that her very first son would be the promised Redeemer – (the Hebrew should be translated: Eve said, 'I have brought forth the LORD-man'). Chapter 4 shows us how sin cannot be contained but spreads and deepens. Cain ignores the lesson of the animal skins and thinks that vegetables are enough for the LORD. Out of jealousy for Abel's animal sacrifice, Cain commits murder.

---

[1] <www.jewsforjesus.org> There are lots of online papers and Bible studies at this site, particularly in the 'Believers' section.

Chapter 5 has been described as a litany of death. Adam died. Seth died. Enosh died. Kenan died. Mahalalel died. Jared died. Methusaleh died. Lamech died. Only Enoch gives hope that humanity is not doomed to be completely swallowed up by the grave.

Further Questions:

1. After Adam and Eve had rebelled against the LORD, whose side does He take?
2. As Adam and Eve are banished from the Garden of God, wrapped in bloody animal skins, sentenced to death and a life of pain and sweat, it is not at all clear how they have become like God. How did their choosing their own way against Christ make them like one of the members of the Trinity (3:22)?
3. Why did the LORD God warn Adam and Eve from eating of the tree of life? Can humanity ever eat from the tree of life? (Revelation 22:2)
4. Why do we have the story of Lamech recorded for us in Genesis 4:19–24?
5. If there had been no sin, there would have been no death or decay in creation at all. In the light of this, why do you think those early humans lived such long lives?

Genesis 3:1-24

There is so much to gain from studying Genesis 3. It tells us a lot about why the world is like it is and we are like we are. The themes of Genesis 3 are picked up time after time throughout the Bible.

Verse 1: Was Satan simply asking for information? How does Satan try to portray the LORD by his question?

Verses 2-3: Did Eve accurately report the words of the LORD?

Verses 4-5: When Satan spoke such a great lie, how could Eve possibly believe him? Was there any truth in his words? How does Satan try to portray the significance of disobedience to the LORD?

Verses 6-7: In what sense were their eyes opened? What caused Eve to take the fruit? What does this say about the root cause of sin?

Verse 8: What kind of relationship did Adam and Eve have with this Divine Person before their sin? How could God come for a walk?

Verses 9-13: Who takes responsibility for this action? Whose fault was it?

Verses 14-15: Why is the Promised Offspring said to be the woman's offspring and not the man's? (Isaiah 7:14) What relationship is going to exist between the serpent and the woman? What future event is described here and how?

Verse 16: What is the contrast between this verse and 2:23-24? What is meant by the word 'desire'? (Cf. 4:7)

Verses 17-19: What do these verses tell us about the seriousness of sin?

Verses 20-24: What signs of hope can we find in these verses? How are the LORD's preventative measures a sign of His grace?

Week of Readings

Sunday:	1 Corinthians 15:20–49
Monday:	Genesis 3
Tuesday:	Genesis 4
Wednesday:	Genesis 5
Thursday:	Ezekiel 28
Friday:	1 John 3:7–24
Saturday:	Psalm 51

4. The Beginning of Judgement

Chapters 6-11

Key Truth: Although evil may seem universal and almighty, causing division and shame, the grace and judgement of God are greater.

1. The Wickedness of Humanity

We saw how Satan first drew humanity into sin, and now we see another example of angelic corruption of humanity. The 'sons of God' were angels (see Job chapter 1) who seduced human women. In 6:4 we see that the children produced from these 'marriages' were strange giants called Nephilim. It seems as if (verse 4) the many legends from different cultures in the world (especially those from ancient Rome and Greece) describing the gods producing heroic offspring with human women) are not referring back to a wonderful golden age, but to an age of gross wickedness[1].

How could humanity have been seduced by such evil? Genesis 6:5 is one of the most sobering verses in the Bible – every inclination of the thoughts of the human heart was only evil all the time. The sin that had been unleashed through Adam and Eve could not be contained or controlled. The human heart is a slave to sin.

What can hurt Almighty God? Grief for the world that He loves causes the Almighty pain. Through Christ, the Father had given such gracious blessings to Adam and Eve. Not only had they neglected Christ's warning, but now the whole human race had plunged into everything that

---

[1] There are a variety of views about the interpretation of these verses in Genesis chapter 6. Some feel that it is describing marriages between believers and unbelievers at the time. Others think it is referring to a genetic line of godly people becoming corrupted as they were mixed with an ungodly genetic line.

God hated. The grief and pain in the heart of God was accompanied with His anger against such sinful corruption. There had to be a reckoning. Justice had to be done.

2. The Safety of the Ark

Only one man, with his family, was found who still trusted in the Promised Seed, therefore he was called a righteous man. Noah was to be a new start for the human race after the coming judgement. The LORD instructed Noah to make an ark, a huge boat. In this boat a selection of all the animals had to be gathered, so that they could survive the coming flood that would wipe out life on earth. Noah had to take seven of every clean animal and two (a male and a female) of every unclean animal. How did Noah gather all these animals together? In 7:8–9 we see that they all just came to Noah, by the mighty power of God.

Noah was looking forward to the LORD-Man, the Seed promised in Genesis 3:15. As such the Ark was such a powerful presentation of the promise of Christ as the place of safety from the ultimate judgement of God.

3. The Extent of Judgement and Grace

The flood was not a local problem. It became embedded in the human memory worldwide, from Indo-China to South America. It is only in Genesis 6–9, however, that we have the original and definitive account of a catastrophe whose impact was universal, never to be repeated. We note that water came up from under the earth as well as deluging down from the sky (Genesis 7:11).

It is important that we meditate on this. 2 Peter 3:3–7 reminds us that the global judgement shown at the flood was a guarantee of the cosmic judgement on the final Day of God when Jesus Christ returns in glory. There was no escape from the judgement of God against sin in Noah's day. The **only** place of safety was the ark, the divinely appointed place of salvation. We see that also in 1 Peter 3:18–22. The ark symbolises the way that we are saved through the death and resurrection of Christ. The experience of the flood and the ark must have deeply reaffirmed Noah's trust in Christ.

In Genesis 8:1 we see that God had not forgotten Noah. His plans for the world had not ended. The ark eventually found a resting place and life on earth began again. Noah's first action was to offer a burnt offering to the LORD, an offering of clean animals, showing Noah's deep understanding of sacrifice. The LORD reaffirms His covenant with the creation. He cannot destroy or curse the world every time human sin runs wild, because then the world would quickly become lifeless and barren. The LORD promised (9:11) that there would never again be a global flood to destroy life on earth. Instead He put a rainbow in the sky in order to remind Him of His permanent covenant with creation.

4. Human Unity and Diversity

We speak about 'the different races' of the world, but actually we are all part of the one human race. Genesis 10:32: 'These are the clans of Noah's sons, according to their lines of descent, within their nations. From these the nations spread out over the earth after the flood.' We can all trace our genealogy back to Adam and Eve, but at the flood, the whole human race narrowed down to just one family again. We are all descendants of Noah as well.

We are given a glimpse into the tremendous gospel faith of the believers before the flood in the New Testament book of Jude verses 14 and 15. Enoch was Noah's great-grandfather and prophesied the Second Coming of the LORD to the ungodly sinners of his generation. We have seen that Noah understood the importance of animal sacrifice and blood. Noah understood these things in terms of the future work of Christ. However, once the human race expanded across the world again, these basic truths were quickly corrupted and we find all kinds of strange blood sacrifices among ancient pagan religions in every part of the world. This reminds us again that all the nations are descendants of Noah.

5. Human Glory and Shame

Humanity was created in the image of God, but we have seen how far below such life humanity can fall. Instead of living the life of God, we so often live the life of Satan. This strange paradox and ambiguity is brought out for us so well in Genesis. In chapter 4:20–22 we saw how the children of Lamech were capable of such greatness: Jabal invented livestock farming; his brother Jubal invented a whole musical tradition; their half-brother Tubal-Cain developed both bronze and iron working. What a family! Their father was a wicked murderer, yet the children are capable of such greatness.

We see the same thing in chapter 10:6–20. Ham was a wicked man, yet his descendants display this strange paradox. We find Cush – presumably the founder of the nation of Egypt (Psalm 68:31). He was the father of a man called Nimrod, a man whose ability in both war and hunting were legendary. He was the stuff of legend, superlative in human ability.

He founded the nations of Babylon, Akkad, and Assyria and built the great city of Nineveh. What ability! Yet, both Egypt and Babylon became symbols of pagan opposition to the gospel throughout the Bible, (Revelation 18:2–3). The height and the depth of humanity! We see this down through history and around us today. Great skill, intelligence, ingenuity, courage and compassion existing alongside greed, unbelief, lust, anger and selfishness – and often all in the same person. If we didn't have this biblical story of creation and fall, we wouldn't be able to understand humanity at all.

6. Human Pride and Confusion

Humanity united in evil is too terrible to bear. The human race gathered together for a building project – a tower that would reach to the heavens. It probably isn't wise to imagine what exactly this tower would have been like – but the goal of the work is clear. The people wanted to 'make a name for themselves' (11:4). They were proud and, much like Lucifer, wanted to lift themselves to the throne of God.

When the LORD came to see this tower He was not pleased. We have already seen how the sinful human heart is only wicked from childhood - if the whole of humanity could unite together in its wickedness then it would be too terrible. The LORD decided to confuse the human race. There would no longer be a common mind and a common understanding[2]. All the people were scattered over the face of the earth. We should remember that the unity of humanity can only be achieved through the gospel of Jesus Christ and the power of the Holy Spirit. Any other basis of unity brings too many dangers.

Further Questions:

1. Given the promise of Genesis 3:15, why were the events of chapter 6:1–4 so dangerous?
2. What happened between Noah and Ham in chapter 9?
3. What do the actions of God in these chapters reveal about His nature?
4. Did it ever rain from Genesis 2:5–6 to Genesis 7:10? Could it be that the reason there had never been rainbows before was that it had never rained before?

---

[2] 11:1 is perhaps better understood as: 'The whole world had one mind and a common understanding'.

Genesis 8:20-9:17

Sometimes we may think of God's gospel as simply concerned with our own individual salvation or just the human race. However, in this next section of Genesis, we are reminded that the gospel of the Messiah concerns the whole creation and all creatures.

Chapter 8, verse 20: Why did Noah kill some animals for the LORD? (Hint: what was the purpose of a **burnt** offering? See Leviticus 1:3–4)

Verses 21–22: Note the contrasts between the LORD's promise here and His judgement in chapter 3:17–19. Is there any difference between the behaviour of mankind before the flood (6:5) and after it?

Chapter 9, verses 1–3: Compare God's blessing here and the blessing of chapter 1:28–30.

Verses 4–7: What is at stake when the blood of mankind is shed according to these verses?[3]

Verses 8–11: What is God's covenant with all living creatures on the earth and how is it fulfilled? Why does He include every member of the animal kingdom?

Verses 12–17: Is the rainbow for us or for the LORD? What does it signify?

---

[3] Notice that even the animals will have to give an accounting for human blood.

Week of Readings

Sunday:	1 Peter 3:8–22; 2 Peter 2:1–14
Monday:	Genesis 6
Tuesday:	Genesis 7
Wednesday:	Genesis 8
Thursday:	Genesis 9
Friday:	Genesis 10
Saturday:	Genesis 11

5. The Beginning of the Church

Chapters 12-16

Key Truth: The whole Christian church looks back to Abraham as the father of the faith.

It has been suggested that the word 'Church' describes the people of God after the Day of Pentecost in Acts, whereas the word 'Israel' describes the people of God before that. However, this is not true to the Bible. In Acts 7:38, Stephen speaks of the 'Church (*ekklesia*) in the desert'. We must always remember that the Church was not born at Pentecost but has existed since the beginning of the world. In the Greek translation of the Old Testament from c. 300 BC, the old Jewish translators chose the Greek word 'ekklesia' (church) to translate the Hebrew word for the Assembly of Israel. Perhaps the NIV chooses the word 'assembly' in Acts 7:38 in order to remind us that when we are reading about the assembly of Israel in the Old Testament we are reading about the Church.

1. Abram's Call

If all the nations have been scattered over the earth, in Abram the LORD begins to gather them back together. Through Abram all the peoples of the earth will be blessed. In chapter 12, verse 7 we see the promise of the Seed (given to Eve) brought back to our attention. The promise of Christ is renewed to Abram and his family (see Galatians 3:16). What are these promises all about? They are focussing on the fact that the human race in every nation will be redeemed through the Seed (the Christ) and that there would be a nation of Israel at the eastern end of the Mediterranean Sea. The fact that the land occurs so often in these promises is reminding those Old Testament saints that the whole creation, the whole universe, will be redeemed at the end on the Day of Christ (see below for more on this). Salvation is not just about souls and spirits. It is about bodies as well. In fact, the whole creation, the animals and the earth itself, will all be liberated from the effects of human sin (Romans 8:18–25).

Abram seems to have some background knowledge because he understands about altars and sacrifice. Notice that the LORD **appeared** to Abram. If we find this a bit confusing, Colossians 1:15 removes all doubt. It was Christ who brought these words and promises to the people of God down through the Bible's history.

Abram's behaviour in Egypt shows us that Abram was not chosen because of his own goodness. Abram was saved only because he trusted in Christ and not because of any goodness in himself.

2. Abram's Choice

Chapter 13 lets us know that Abraham understood the real significance of the Promised Land. It would have been very easy to have become fixed on the land of Canaan as the most exciting thing in Abram's future. Inheriting such a fertile and strategic bit of the world would overwhelm most of us. However, Abraham knew that it was just a sign of the infinitely greater inheritance that we will receive at the end of the world on Resurrection morning. Abraham could have built a city or at least become part of the politics and cultural life of the Canaanite cities. Instead, he lived in tents and allowed Lot, his nephew, first pick of the land.

Hebrews 11:8–10: 'By faith Abraham, when called to go to a place he would later receive as his inheritance, obeyed and went, even though he did not know where he was going. By faith he made his home in the Promised Land like a stranger in a foreign country; he lived in tents, as did Isaac and Jacob, who were heirs with him of the same promise. For he was looking forward to the city with foundations, whose architect and builder is God.'

3. Abram's Tithe

Lot was a righteous man (2 Peter 2:7), but he had made bad choices. Even though the men of Sodom were enemies of the LORD, Lot got caught up in the life and business of these pagan cities. He found himself a victim of the wars between these pagan kings (14:12).

Abram, with his impressively large household, had to rescue Lot. The King of Sodom wanted to make a deal with Abram, forming an alliance. However, before the king of Sodom arrived Abram was met by a priest-king called Melchizedek. He gave Abram bread and wine. He was the priest of God Most High (a title normally reserved for God the Father). Abram gave Melchizedek a tenth of everything he had. Who is this Melchizedek? Some think he was simply an ordinary man who has a mysterious place in the Bible. Others have wondered if this was the pre-incarnate Christ Himself. Melchizedek means 'king of righteousness' and 'king of Salem' means 'king of peace'. Certainly, when we read Hebrews chapter 7 it does look as if it was the Son of God appearing in a special way. Who apart from the Eternal Son is the everlasting, immortal priest between the Father and humanity?

After this meeting with Melchizedek, Abram knows that he cannot form an alliance with any of the pagan kings. He has a King above all earthly kings, a King who will give him an inheritance far, far greater than anything available to the king of Sodom.

4. Abram's Faith

Chapter 15 is one of the most quoted parts of the Bible. It is the time when Abram's righteousness is clearly explained. The Word of the LORD came to Abram in a vision making sure that Abram understood the relationship between them. The Word of the LORD (Christ) was Abram's reward – more than any land or children or influence.

Notice how this passage shows clearly that the Word of the LORD is a distinct person. In verse 4 the Word of the LORD visits Abram. In verse 5 it says, '**He** took him (Abram) outside and said … Then **He** said to him (Abram)'. The Word of the LORD is a **He**! It is crucial that we recognise that it is the Eternal Christ who is speaking to Abram here because of verse 6, 'Abram believed the LORD, and He credited it to him as righteousness.' Abram believed the One who was speaking to him. Abram trusted Christ. Of course, this was Christ long before He became one of us through the virgin – but it was the Second Person of the Trinity nonetheless.

This is so important because Genesis 15:6 is the model of Christian faith throughout the Bible. Abram didn't just believe in 'God' in a general sense. He believed in Christ specifically; Christ who set the gospel promises in front of Abram.

An unusual Gospel picture is performed in chapter 15, whereby the LORD solemnly seals His gospel promises to Abram. Abram could take no active part as the LORD confirms 'for certain' what He will do for Abraham.

5. Abram's Son

Abram's first son was Ishmael. Sarai and Abram had been waiting for the child that the LORD had promised them. Time was moving on and they were both very old. Surely the LORD needed some practical help here? Perhaps it was time to take matters into their own hands. Abram and Sarai hatch a scheme to produce the promised child through their own efforts by taking advantage of Sarai's servant Hagar (16:1–2). Abram married Hagar and Ishmael is conceived.

Sarai and Abram ill-treat Hagar, who was forced to run away. Hagar was a pregnant woman, on her own in the desert without any resources. Things did not look very good. Yet, Christ had not forgotten Hagar: 'The Angel of the LORD found Hagar…'. The word 'angel' simply means 'messenger' or 'one who is sent'. The Angel of the LORD simply means 'The One Sent from the LORD'[1]. It is exciting to see some of the times when Christ appears as The Angel of the LORD – Genesis 16:7–11, 21:17, 22:11–15, 31:11; Exodus 3:1–6, 14:19; Numbers 22:21–35; Judges 2:1–4, 6:11–24, 13:1–25; 1 Kings 19:1–18; Psalm 34:7–9 and others.

The Angel of the LORD is the LORD (verse 13). Hagar knows that she has met God and tells The Angel of the LORD 'You are the God who sees me. I have now seen the One who sees me.'

She sees God! Although God the Father cannot be seen (we know this from John 1:18), we find that many people have seen God the Son in the Old Testament. Colossians 1:15 – Christ is the image; the visible form, of the invisible God.

Further Questions:

1. In Genesis 12:8 Abram calls on the Name of the LORD (Yahweh/ Jehovah). In Exodus 6:3 it seems as if the name of the LORD was not known to Abram. What is the answer to this? (Note: there is a helpful footnote in the NIV.[2])
2. What are the arguments for and against Melchizedek being Christ? (Cf. Psalm 110)
3. Is it right to speak of the Old Testament as 'before Christ'?

---

[1] In the Gospels, Jesus often describes Himself as the One sent from the Father, the One sent to do His will (John 3:17, 5:23, 6:38, 8:29, 12:49, etc). If we have understood the truth about the Angel of the LORD, then we begin to appreciate what Jesus is saying.

[2] Alternative translation – 'By my name the LORD did I not let myself be known to them?'

Genesis 15:1-21

This chapter is one of the most important in the whole Bible because it is here that we are explicitly shown that Abram is righteous before the LORD because he believes in the Promised Messiah.

Verses 1-3: Why did Abram need to be reassured in this way? Why was he afraid?

Verses 4-5: Why does the Word of the LORD (Christ) take Abram outside to look at the stars?

Verse 6: What is the significance of the word 'credited' (Cf. Romans 6:23)?

Verses 7-12: Abram is told to bring a selection of clean animals before the LORD and cut them all in half. In the Old Testament, covenants are described as being 'cut' rather than written. How does this help us to understand this strange ritual?

Verses 13-16: Make a list of the things that are prophesied here and consider how they were fulfilled.

Verses 16-21: What are we to think about those people who were living in the land promised to Abram's descendants?

Week of Readings

Sunday:	Galatians 3:1–25
Monday:	Genesis 12
Tuesday:	Genesis 13
Wednesday:	Genesis 14
Thursday:	Genesis 15
Friday:	Genesis 16
Saturday:	Romans 4:1–25

6. The Beginning of the Sacraments

Chapters 17-24

Key Truth: The LORD God has always shown His gospel in down-to-earth forms.

The word 'sacrament' isn't in the Bible – it is a word that Christians have used down the years to describe those physical actions that the LORD has commanded us to perform in order to present the gospel of the Messiah. Today, of course, we simply have baptism and the LORD's Supper. But the Old Testament is full of other symbolic actions that prophesied the Messiah.

1. A Sign of Justification by Faith

The LORD appeared to Abram again, when he was 99 years old (17:1). He visited Abram in order to confirm the covenant that He had made with him. Abram's name is changed to **Abraham** in order to mark this event.

We have come across the word 'covenant' several times. Sometimes people think of it as a kind of contract in which God and humanity negotiate an agreement. God's covenant is nothing like that. God the Father through God the Son established this covenant without any input from humanity at all. He has confirmed it on many occasions. When the Bible speaks at different times of God making a covenant with various people, we might think that He has lots of different covenants. However, when we look at what each of these 'covenants' describe we see that there is just one covenant, the gospel of the Christ (The Seed). Even Adam was determined by that one covenant of God which stretches right back to creation itself – Hosea 6:7 and Jeremiah 33:19-20.

God's covenant in Christ is not a list of demands, but a gift of promises in Christ. Those who trust in Christ, whether in the Old or New

Testament, show that they trust in Christ by behaving in the way that the covenant describes. We do not earn the free gift of the covenant – but we respond to it with love and service.

The visible LORD makes unconditional promises to Abram (Genesis 17:1–8). Abraham's response to these promises is to circumcise males when they are 8 days old. This physical sign marked them as members of the covenant people.[1]

Notice that the sign can be given to foreigners as well as native Abrahamites. The covenant community was for anybody in the world who trusted in the Promised Seed. Ishmael receives this mark as well, but is told in verse 21 that he would not be the ancestor of the Seed. Ishmael had to submit to his younger brother, a brother who had not yet even been born, in order to be part of the covenant people.

2. A Sign of Divine Fellowship

Genesis 18 has always been one of the most fascinating chapters throughout history. There have been many religious paintings depicting this meal between Abram and the LORD. Because it talks of 'three men' arriving at Abraham's tent many Christians have thought of this as the Trinity visiting Abraham. However, no one has ever seen the Father at any time. Rather, when we read the story carefully (notice 19:1), we see that it is the LORD plus two angels.

Abraham is very excited by this visit. He rushes around making sure everything is prepared to the highest possible standards. He gets them water for their feet and serves up a meal as they sit under one of the great trees of Mamre.

In the generations following the apostles this chapter was often debated because many non-Christians worshipped a god who could never have such direct interaction with the physical world – eating meals and washing feet! However, the Christians pointed out that this is just the way the Living God always acts. The Father said that the creation was 'very good' and the Son walked in His Garden, having all kinds of direct interaction with His people, until finally He became one of us to become a citizen of planet earth. We look forward to the time when the dwelling of God will come out of heaven to be on earth forevermore (Revelation 21:2–4).

---

[1] Why not women as well? Many have said that women already had such a sign of blood in the menstrual cycle. The Old Testament signs were all marked by blood. The New Testament sign of membership of the covenant people is, of course, baptism (see Colossians 2:9–12)

Abraham's meal was a sign of the warm friendship between the Creator and His creatures. It was over that meal that Abraham could discuss the future of Sodom with the God who was his friend. The LORD would not hide His actions from Abraham (verses 17–19).

Notice also how, in verses 20–21, the LORD wants to see at first-hand the wickedness of Sodom and Gomorrah. The Living God cares so much about His world that He governs it in a hands-on way. This is why Abraham knows that in asking for mercy on Sodom and Gomorrah he is not running against the nature of his LORD.

3. A Sign of Everlasting Judgement

There were not even ten righteous people in Sodom and Gomorrah. Only Lot's family are covenant people. When the two angels arrive, Lot offers them hospitality (19:2). He knows how dangerous the city square is. All the men of the city, both young and old, want to rape the two angels.

Lot had bought a house in Sodom instead of living in a tent nearby (cf. 13:12). This has clearly deeply compromised his discipleship. He thinks that allowing his daughters to be raped is an acceptable way of protecting the angels! (Lot is a warning about how easily our judgement of good and evil can wither away in bad company.) The angels were quite capable of looking after themselves and they simply blinded all the men. The angels protect Lot and his family from the coming judgement, taking them out of the city before the judgement falls. Lot's wife had not given up her life in Sodom and she looked back even as it was being destroyed.

Genesis 19:24 is one of the great verses of the whole book – there are two LORDs in the one verse! The LORD on earth rains down burning sulphur from the LORD in the heavens. Whenever we meet Jehovah's Witnesses we should ask them which of these LORDs they are witnessing to!

Even though Lot and his daughters escaped, yet the compromise and sin of Sodom was still with them. Lot could easily be led into drunkenness and immorality by his immoral daughters.

4. A Sign of God's Grace

Abraham was also a compromised man. He was certainly not saved because of his good works! Even though he knew how much trouble could come by lying about Sarah (see 12:10–20), yet he makes the same mistake again with Abimelech (20:2). God's continued faithfulness to Abraham and Sarah is an enduring testimony to his grace.

So, because of this covenant faithfulness, the LORD God 'was gracious to Sarah as He had said, and the LORD did for Sarah what he had promised' (21:1). The next physical sign of the gospel was a baby, Isaac. Isaac was the miraculous baby, produced from Abraham and Sarah when it was impossible.

Ishmael did not like Isaac. He didn't like the attention Isaac was receiving when he, Ishmael, was the elder brother. There was more to this than just sibling rivalry – it was a gospel matter. Ishmael represented what could be produced through human effort. He was the result of Abraham and Sarah taking matters into their own hands with Hagar. When Ishmael refused to submit to Isaac, it was clear to Sarah that this was a spiritual issue – and God agreed with Sarah when Abraham prayed about it. If Ishmael inherited Abraham's blessing then human effort (Ishmael) would have beaten God's grace (Isaac). This is why Hagar and Ishmael have to be thrown out. It is the first example of church discipline!

It is important that we make these connections, because that is how the apostle Paul explains the incident in Galatians 4:21–31. It is exciting to see that Paul is simply paying attention to what is actually said in this incident rather than reading in New Testament ideas. Paul is a model given by the Holy Spirit to teach us how to understand the Bible.

5. A Sign of Substitution

Abraham is told to go and sacrifice his son Isaac in the region of Moriah. This is the place where the temple of Jerusalem would be built hundreds of years later, and most importantly, the very place where Jesus would be crucified – see 2 Chronicles 3:1. Abraham didn't take any time to deliberate. He set off early the next day. It takes three days to get to Moriah, and then Abraham says something very striking to his servants - "Stay here with the donkey while I and the boy go over there. We will worship and then we will come back to you." Abraham knew that although he was intending to kill Isaac, yet they would both come back alive. Hebrews 11:17–19. Perhaps more than anybody else in the Bible Abraham is allowed to experience God the Father's side of the Cross of Christ – giving up his beloved son.

Abraham finds a ram and sacrifices that instead. But, where was the promised lamb that Abraham spoke of in verse 8? The Lamb of God was not going to be sacrificed on that mountain for nearly 2,000 years. Abraham looked forward to that death of Christ when he called the mountain 'The LORD Will Provide' – verse 14. The ram had taken Isaac's place, but the blood of animals never took away anybody's sin. The real substitute was that Lamb of God that Abraham set his faith on.

6. A Sign of the Future

Abraham grieved deeply when Sarah died (23:2). They had certainly been through a great deal together. In order to make a gospel statement about this death, Abraham decided to buy a tomb. He wanted one part of the Promised Land – the cave and field of Machpelah – as a guaranteed possession for his descendants. There is some genuine humour in this story. The Hittites speak as if they want to simply give Abraham the field as a gift – yet it is clear that it is really a business negotiation. It is a little insight into the business practices of the day! This field and this tomb are not forgotten. We will see them again at the end of Genesis.

Abraham wanted to secure a wife for Isaac. He did not want Isaac to marry one of the pagan women of Canaan. The Bible is full of warnings against Christians marrying non-Christians. Abraham sends his servant away to find a relative for Isaac to marry. The servant goes to the family of Abraham's brother, Nahor. This was quite a family. Not only is Rebekah from that family, but Elihu, the only person in the book of Job who really understands the truth, is also descended from Nahor. Not every member of this great family is truly godly (Laban for example seems compromised with his household gods – Genesis 31:19), but they all know of the LORD. The servant asks for some miraculous guidance to help him know who is the right person for Isaac to marry. Perhaps because the issue is of such importance this miraculous guidance is promptly given. At first the story seems a bit misogynist, with Rebekah being traded almost like a horse - but, at the end of the story it is clear that ultimately the matter is her decision (Genesis 24:57–58).

Further Questions:

1. It must have been amazing to have enjoyed a meal with the Eternal Christ like Abraham did in Genesis 18. Why can't that sort of thing happen right now?
2. How could God ask Abraham to do something so bad in Genesis 22?
3. Why is there so much concern about where a person is buried in the books of Genesis and Exodus?
4. Why is God in His Word so against Christians marrying non-Christians? (Cf. 1 Kings 11:1–8)
5. In Colossians chapter 2:11–12, it looks as if both circumcision and baptism are physical actions that refer to being born again in Christ. Why do you think the LORD replaced circumcision with baptism?

Genesis 22:1-19

It has been said that Genesis 22 provides the background for everything else that we will read in the books of Moses. The Seed has been promised several times but it is in this chapter that Abraham identifies where the Seed will accomplish His work of redemption.

Verses 1-2: Bearing in mind the existence of Ishmael, how can God describe Isaac as Abraham's only son? What similarities are there here with the way God the Father describes his Son later on?

Verses 3-8: The regulations detailing the burnt offering were not spelt out in detail until at least Exodus 27:1-8 (if not Leviticus 1) yet Abraham and Isaac both seem to know what is involved. What does this tell us about the understanding of the patriarchs? How do these verses demonstrate that Abraham believed in the resurrection?

Verses 9-12: In what ways do Isaac's actions mirror those of Christ? (Cf. Isaiah 53, esp. verse 7)

Verses 13-14: Why does Abraham offer a ram and not a lamb? (Cf. verse 8) How do we know that Abraham was still looking forward to what God would do?

Verses 15-19: How do the promises of the LORD in these verses compare to His previous promises to Abraham? What does Abraham's return to Beersheba signify? (Cf. 21:31-34)

Week of Readings

Sunday:	John 19:16–30
Monday:	Genesis 17 and 18
Tuesday:	Genesis 19 and 20
Wednesday:	Genesis 21 and 22
Thursday:	Genesis 23 and 24
Friday:	John 1:19–37
Saturday:	Luke 22:14–30

7. The Beginning of Election

Chapters 25-31

Key Truth: Jacob shows us that we can never earn the favour of the Living God through our own schemes.

1. A Stew for a Birthright

After Abraham's vigour had been miraculously restored back in chapter 15, Abraham had enjoyed ever increasing fertility (25:2). Certainly with his new wife Keturah he is able to produce many children. When Abraham died he was buried in the tomb he had purchased for Sarah.

Ishmael had prospered, but the story now zooms in upon Isaac's children, Jacob and Esau. Rebekah had been barren, but in answer to Isaac's prayer she conceived. It was a difficult pregnancy. The twins wrestled within her. When she asked the LORD about this, He gave the key statement about these two babies, the statement that would explain their lives and destinies: 'Two nations are in your womb, and two peoples from within you will be separated; one people will be stronger than the other, and the older will serve the younger.' Who is the stronger? Why must the older serve the younger? Why does God choose Jacob rather than Esau?

The two babies were born, but were strikingly different. Jacob was quiet and domesticated, but a manipulative and scheming man. Esau was the outdoor type and very straightforward in his social interactions. Isaac, predictably, loves Esau more than Jacob.

Esau was more concerned with the immediate hunger pains he had after hunting. Jacob had his eye on his schemes and long-term future. He bribed Esau with a mere stew. That incident summarises the two men. Esau was shortsighted and impulsive. Jacob was manipulative and scheming.

2. A Well for Water

In Genesis 26 the LORD appeared to Isaac (verse 2). It was not the time for going down to Egypt yet, but Isaac received confirmation of his own position as the ancestor of Christ. The promises, with the sign of the land, were refreshed to Isaac.

Isaac picked up the bad habits of his father, because he lied about Rebekah in the same way that Abraham had done on two occasions about Sarah. At first Abimelech seemed to welcome Isaac but when he saw how powerful and wealthy Isaac became, the Philistines wanted Isaac to leave them alone. Eventually Isaac found a place to live, and at Beersheba the LORD appeared to him once again, to reassure him after all the trouble with the Philistines. Isaac's servants dug a good well and Abimelech made a peaceful agreement with Isaac. The striking thing is that the Philistines do not join up with Isaac as followers of the LORD. The Philistines seemed to know about the LORD, yet they just wanted a quiet life.

The chapter ends with bad news about Esau. He decided to marry not just one but two Hittite women. It is no wonder that he was a source of grief to Isaac and Rebekah (26:35).

3. A Goatskin for a Blessing

However, Jacob was also a problem child. Isaac thought that he was about to die (27:2), so he wanted to give his blessing to Esau. The fact that Esau had lost his birthright to Jacob seems to have been forgotten or ignored by Isaac and Esau. Jacob had not forgotten, and with Rebekah's help he takes the blessing away from Esau.

Isaac was easily won by good food. Isaac must have known what the LORD had said about these two boys, that the older must serve the younger, but he preferred Esau. Jacob, the Schemer, had no difficulty lying to his father and convincing him to give him the blessing. The blessing that Isaac had received from Abraham was passed on to Jacob.

However, Esau arrived with his freshly prepared meat. As soon as Isaac realised what had happened he 'trembled violently'. He had tried to overcome the LORD's prophecy about his sons, but now he realised it was impossible. The LORD's choice cannot be changed or resisted. Esau begged for a blessing too, but Isaac would not change his mind. Isaac could easily have simply revoked all that he had said to Jacob, but he knew what the LORD had said. Isaac would not change his mind even though Esau begged him (see Hebrews 12:16–17).

So, what could Isaac give Esau? He reminded Esau of what the LORD had said about the two boys – about Esau serving Jacob. Although Isaac feared that Esau would not be able to put up with this, yet if Esau had only listened and submitted to the LORD's choice of Jacob then he too could have been part of that covenant people. The LORD's election of Jacob did not rule Esau out – but Esau had to humble himself and trust the Promised Messiah in spite of Jacob's lying and scheming. However, Esau would not submit to scheming Jacob and bore a grudge against him. Jacob had to run away to live with Rebekah's brother Laban. Isaac acknowledged Jacob at the beginning of chapter 28 and gave him the marriage advice that he had received from Abraham – do not marry pagan women. Esau heard about that and went to marry a daughter of Ishmael as well as the wives he already had (28:9).

4. A Stone for a Pillow

After all of Jacob's lies and deceit we might be tempted to think that he could not be of any use in Christ's dealings with humanity. However, as Jacob was on the run to Laban, he stopped for a sleep and gathered some stones for a pillow (28:11). While he was sleeping he saw a stairway between heaven and earth. The angels of God were travelling between heaven and earth on the stairway. Jacob, for the first time in his life, saw the LORD, standing at the top of the stairway.[1] The LORD who joins heaven and earth renewed the promises to Jacob, adding a personal note assuring Jacob of His care for him.

When Jacob woke up he realised that this was an important place. He set up a memorial stone and called the place Bethel. Did this incident have a big impact on Jacob? Did his life change from this point on? No, he remained the same old scheming Jacob. He did not submit to the LORD who so graciously appeared to him. Instead, in 28:20–22 Jacob tried again to bargain with the LORD for the LORD's favour. Jacob was only prepared to accept conditional submission, even at this stage of his life.

5. Seven Years for a Wife

Jacob arrived at Laban's house and fell in love with Laban's daughter Rachel and started helping out straightaway (29:10). However, in meeting Laban, Jacob had met his match. Laban was just as devious and crafty as Jacob. He even managed to trick Jacob into marrying Leah as well as Rachel.

---

[1] It was Christ, who is the link between heaven and earth – as Jesus said in John 1:51.

Jacob was very blessed with children from Leah and Rachel. All his sons were gracious gifts from the LORD, not produced by any of Jacob's schemes, another sign pointing Jacob to the LORD's graciousness and faithfulness. There were all kinds of intrigues among Jacob and his two wives as these children are produced, but none of it was necessary. The LORD had promised to bless them, so that they did not need to keep trying to sort it all out in their own strength.

The most striking example of this is Jacob's efforts in breeding Laban's flocks (30:25–43). When we read how Jacob made a strange deal to get the speckled animals and how he had got a strange scheme for making the animals produce such colouration we may well be a little bemused. Could Jacob really change the animals' genetics by stripping the bark off some branches? It all becomes clearer when we read 31:10–13. The LORD was the one who had produced these breeding results – but as always Jacob thought it was all down to his clever ideas.

6. A Heap for a Witness

Rachel stole her father's household gods and they all fled (31:20). As usual Jacob left under a cloud of deceit and scheming.

Laban, Jacob and Rachel all have their own schemes when Laban finally catches up with them. The life of Jacob is one long tale of sinful plans. Finally Jacob and Laban have to make a deal to stay away from each other. Even Laban has become weary of Jacob, so they set up a heap of stones to mark their agreement. They ask the LORD to keep them apart.[2] Far from being a great witness to the LORD's covenant Jacob continued to live his own way, fighting against Christ who patiently and graciously watches over Jacob. Jacob still did not submit to the Angel of the LORD – he still trusted in his own schemes.

Further Questions:

1. Why did God choose Jacob rather than Esau? Jacob is much more deceitful and scheming than Esau. Surely Esau was a much more promising person?
2. What are we to think about the sexual mess that these men get into with their many wives? Genesis 2:23-25 seems a long time ago after these chapters!
3. Why is there so much about the life of Jacob in Genesis? Do we really need this amount of information about such a difficult character?

---

[2] Notice how the LORD has the title 'The Fear of Isaac' in 31:53.

Genesis 25:19-34

The birth of Jacob and Esau is recalled throughout the rest of Scripture as one of the best explanations of the nature of the gospel. The way of the Messiah is not based on genetics or human ways of judging people – it is simply the way of dependence on God's choice and grace.

Verses 19-20: How long did Isaac and Rebekah have to wait for a child? (Cf. verse 26)

Verses 21-22: How do these verses demonstrate that this entire episode is the work of God?

Verse 23: Why did the LORD make this distinction concerning the boys before they were even born? Isn't this unfair? (Cf. Romans 9:10-13)

Verses 24-26: Why were the twins so different from each other? What is the significance of Jacob grasping Esau's heel as he was born?

Verses 29-34: What do we learn about Esau's attitude toward life? What do we learn about the way Jacob tries to obtain greatness?

Week of Readings

Sunday: Genesis 31

Monday: Genesis 25

Tuesday: Genesis 26

Wednesday: Genesis 27

Thursday: Genesis 28

Friday: Genesis 29

Saturday: Genesis 30

8. The Beginning of Israel

Chapters 32-35

Key Truth: Jacob continued to resist and deceive in spite of continued divine grace.

1. Bribing Esau

We have learned so much about the way that Jacob approached life, continually trusting in his own powers of scheming in everything he did. So, when he eventually had to face Esau he approached the whole incident as a test of his negotiating ability. Jacob's life was filled with the presence and care of the LORD, yet he remained self-dependent. Notice how he prepared to meet Esau (32:3–5). Jacob would have held a grudge for decades and decades – therefore he imagines that Esau has been nursing his grudge for all this time. So, Jacob has an elaborate plan involving servants going on ahead at intervals bringing more and more bribes for Esau – see chapter 32:20.

2. Wrestling with God

Jacob had sent all his family and all his possessions and all his servants across the Jabbok river. Now he was alone (32:22–24). Perhaps now he would face up to his life of trusting in his own abilities and yield to Christ, trusting only in Him.

A 'man who is God' comes to wrestle with Jacob through the night. Perhaps no one in the whole Old Testament ever experiences such an intimate time with the second Person of the Trinity, such a direct and physical encounter. Yet the first thing we learn (verse 25) is that Jacob will not yield to Him even at this time. In the Bible the night-time is the time of testing (for example Psalm 17:3). Jacob is tested all night but he will not relent. At daybreak the God-Man wishes to break off the wrestling, but Jacob wished to get something out of the battle. Jacob receives a new name – Israel. Yet, Jacob is still called Jacob. It is as if he does not accept the new name he has been given. Jacob still trusts in himself to gain his own identity.

Jacob realised what had happened. He had seen God face to face. Surely such an incredible night would shake him out of his pattern of life. Jacob remained Jacob and was not yet ready to be Israel. But there was an impact on Jacob – Joseph was still a young boy and Benjamin was yet to be born. We see how these two sons had a better upbringing than the others did.

3. Lying to Esau

Finally Jacob meets Esau (33:1). Jacob was still busy with his plans when Esau rushed to embrace him. For Esau Jacob's double-dealing and tricks are long gone. Esau was a man who couldn't be bothered with grudges. He was simply overjoyed to see his brother again.

Jacob spoke to Esau with fawning words, full of apparent humility. He addressed Esau as 'my lord' and insisted that Esau took the gifts he offered. Jacob had just seen the face of God, but told Esau that his face is just like God's! (verse 10). Was Jacob sincere? No, because although Esau wanted them to join together Jacob goes back to his lying and deceit to avoid seeing Esau again.

4. Deceiving the Shechemites

Genesis chapter 34 is one of the most disturbing chapters in the book. The chapter begins with Dinah, the daughter of Leah and Jacob, being raped by Shechem, one of the pagan men of the area. The big issue that we are faced with in this chapter is this: how will the people defined by the gospel, the grace of God in Christ, respond to this sin committed against them? Are they really gospel people or not?

The first thing that strikes us is how little attention is given to Dinah. That makes us concerned straight away. What was her view of it all? Shechem did love her, but he had acted wickedly towards her. His father, Hamor, who was a local ruler, did not try to cover it all up. He came to speak with Jacob about it straight away. Hamor and Shechem were prepared to pay any price to win the hand of Dinah in marriage.

Jacob knew that his sons would be full of schemes of vengeance so he waited in silence for them to come home. They followed the way of their father (verse 13) by answering deceitfully. This deceit was particularly offensive. Abraham had made it very clear that there could be no marriage with the surrounding pagans, unless of course they converted into gospel covenant people. Circumcision had been given as the sign that the blessings of God's gospel-covenant would be given to people from every nation on earth. Foreigners could join the family of Abraham through circumcision – as we saw in chapter 17. The really wicked deceit by Jacob's sons in 34:13–17 was that they turned circumcision into a sign of them joining up with the Canaanites. They offered to become 'one people' with the Hivites (verse 16), reversing the very meaning of the sign[1].

The plan pleased the pagans. Hamor and Shechem easily persuade their neighbours to go along with the scheme – the Abrahamites seemed very friendly and they had lots of wealth which would all become part of Hivite society. So, all the men were circumcised. Simeon and Levi waited until the men were struggling with pain from the circumcisions and then went into the Hivite city to kill all the men. Then they took all the women and children, all the money and possessions of the Hivites away. What evil irony! They were outraged that Shechem had taken what he wanted by force, but that is exactly what **they** had done, and they had captured many women rather than just one.

What a terrible mess! The covenant people had become famous, not for mercy, justice, compassion and love – but for cruelty, deception, vengeance and plundering. The Canaanites were not being won for Christ – they were being driven away from the Promised Seed. Can this be the people who are going to bless all the nations? Do these people really trust in Christ at all?

5. Returning to Bethel

Once again the LORD had to sort this mess out. He told Jacob to go back to Bethel to get things sorted out. Jacob's speech (35: 2–4) is quite scary. His household is nothing like a godly covenant household. It is full of foreign gods. Their clothing seems to be pagan as well. They have strayed far from the gospel of the Promised Seed. This was a family of unbelief rather than a family of faith.

Notice that the LORD made all the Canaanites terrified of them – so that there is no revenge for the atrocity of chapter 34.

After Jacob built the altar at Bethel, God **appeared** to him. God tries once again to call Jacob to repentance and faith, to a new birth in Christ –

---

[1] It was no wonder the Hivites/Gibeonites later deceitfully tried to join Israel after this incident! (Joshua 9 and 10)

'Your name is Jacob, but you will no longer be called Jacob; your name will be Israel' (verse 10). The LORD had already changed his name to Israel back in chapter 32 – but Jacob had remained as Jacob. Now Jacob is challenged again to accept his new name and character from the Angel of the LORD. Jacob receives a kind of sermon outlining the great covenant promises that had been given to Abraham and Isaac – verses 11–12. How could Jacob wrestle against such gracious persuasion? Yet, the chapter ends with him still called Jacob. He may have carried out some religious rituals to mark the spot, but he still refused to give his life and identity to Christ.

Further Questions:

1. In what ways does Esau prove himself to be a "better" person than Jacob? What does this tell us about the LORD's decision making?
2. Throughout these chapters, Jacob has many encounters and conversations with the LORD, yet he still fails to trust the LORD? How is this repeated today?
3. How do we see the prophecy of 25:23 working out in chapter 36 (see esp. verses 6, 31).
4. Why did the LORD persist with Jacob and his family?

Genesis 32:22-32

Much art and literature has been inspired by this chapter of Scripture. The eighteenth-century Christian, Isaac Watts, described Charles Wesley's hymn about Jacob wrestling with Christ as the greatest hymn ever written.

Verses 22–24a: What was Jacob's state of mind at this time (cf. 32:7)? Where should he have turned for help and support in light of 31:13? Why did Jacob send all his family and his possessions away from him?

Verses 24b–25: How does this encounter reflect the life of Jacob to this point? How does the Man demonstrate He is more powerful than Jacob is?

Verses 26–27: Why is Jacob so insistent on receiving the blessing of this Man? How does he go about trying to obtain this blessing? For whose benefit is the question of verse 27 asked?

Verses 28–29: What does Jacob actually receive and what does this indicate? In what sense has Jacob 'overcome'? Why is Jacob's question of verse 29 so strange and what does this indicate?

Verses 30–31: Who does Jacob think he has been wrestling with? What does verse 1 of chapter 33 indicate about Jacob's response to his encounter with the God?

Week of Readings

Sunday:	Psalm 105
Monday:	Genesis 32
Tuesday:	Genesis 33
Wednesday:	Genesis 34
Thursday:	Genesis 35
Friday:	Genesis 36
Saturday:	Hosea 11:12–12:14

9. The Beginning of Exile

Chapters 36-47

Key Truth: The Israelites are clearly not yet ready to live as God's people in the Promised Land and they end up in a pagan nation – but God intended it all for good.

Before we launch into the epic story of Joseph we are given an account of Esau and all his descendants. Edom and the Edomites crop up many times in the Bible and it is crucial that we understand who these people are and how they relate to Israel. The people of Edom are the brothers of the Israelites – and are never far from the life of Israel.

Genesis 37 verse 1 tells us that Jacob lived in the land of Canaan - but this was soon to change. The one great truth we have learnt in the story of Jacob is that the covenant people are not yet ready to populate the Promised Land. Most of them are not trusting in the Promised Seed. The faithfulness of Abraham seems a distant memory. The next ten chapters involve the movement of all these covenant people from the Promised Land to Egypt. At first it seems a great tragedy, but by the end we see that it is all part of the LORD's purposes. The children of Abraham need to learn some basic gospel lessons before they are ready to live in the land again. They are exiled from the Promised Land for 400 years.

1. Joseph Sold into Slavery

It all begins in chapter 37. Joseph had been having some dreams which understandably irritate the other brothers. Little did they know how true these dreams would turn out to be. However, we have seen how violent and cruel these brothers can be and this wickedness is turned against Joseph. Although they were going to kill him, Judah persuaded them to sell him as a slave into Egypt. While Joseph began his new life as a slave in Egypt, Jacob mourned for his son.

2. Judah Caught in Hypocrisy

The disturbing diagnosis of the unbelief and sin of Jacob's family goes on. If we had any doubts about the need for an exile in Egypt, all such doubts will have been dispelled by the end of chapter 38.

Judah went to marry a Canaanite woman. Judah was so lost in unbelief and sin that he no longer cared for the life of the covenant people. His firstborn son, Er, embraced the Canaanite lifestyle so much that the LORD had to kill him. His other son Onan was also a selfish and wicked man and the LORD killed him as well. It seems as if the sins of God's people have so grieved the LORD that He has very little patience for these sinful children. Tamar, who had been the wife of both Er and Onan, was now in a difficult position. She had to wait for another of Judah's sons to grow up – but given how wicked Judah's sons were, she wasn't very hopeful.

Even when the third son, Shelah, had grown up, Judah didn't let her marry him (verse 14). So, she disguised herself as a prostitute and waited for Judah. Judah had no hesitation in sleeping with a prostitute (another sign of his unbelief and sin). Tamar had her wits about her and took Judah's seal and cord as a guarantee of proper payment.

When Tamar was found to be pregnant, Judah flew into a self-righteous rage. Verse 24 is shocking; 'Bring her out and have her burned to death!' How can a man who has behaved so immorally speak like this? Tamar was ready. She simply produced his seal and cord to expose Judah's hypocrisy.

Judah had chosen to live among the pagans, turning his back on the LORD. There can be no conquest or evangelization of the Promised Land when the covenant people were as full of unbelief as the native Canaanites.

3. Pharaoh Troubled by his Dreams

We might have thought that Joseph's abduction to Egypt was a tragedy, but after we have seen how Judah was living we realise that life in the Promised Land is the very opposite of what it should be. There was no witness to the nations going on from the other eleven brothers. They were being won over to the Canaanites rather than the other way round. Could it be that the Joseph who was all on his own in a pagan nation might be more faithful to the gospel-covenant than the rest?

The LORD was with Joseph, far from the Promised Land in Egypt. Joseph was a great witness to the LORD in Potiphar's house. Potiphar knew about the LORD (39 verse 3) so Joseph had clearly done a good job of speaking about the gospel in his workplace (a model to us all).

Joseph was good-looking and Potiphar's wife fancied him. When he wouldn't go along with her seduction, she falsely accused him and he was put in prison. Surely, now Joseph's life was finished - but the LORD remained faithful to him (39:21). The contrast between Judah in the Promised Land and Joseph in the pagan land is extreme.

While in the prison, the LORD gave Joseph the charismatic gift of interpreting dreams. This was shown to Pharaoh's chief butler ('cupbearer', NIV), who eventually (two years later) remembered Joseph when the Pharaoh had a dream that was troubling him. The Egyptian magicians, with all their occult power, could not tell Pharaoh what his dream had meant. When Joseph was summoned, the LORD enabled him to both describe the dream and give the proper interpretation. Joseph was so faithful in his explanation that even the pagan Pharaoh could see that Joseph was full of the Holy Spirit (41:38).

Joseph was put in charge of the whole of Egypt, preparing for the coming famine. His preparations went so well that people from all over the world came to buy food from Egypt. Joseph, as a faithful covenant child of Abraham, was being an amazing blessing to the nations. The provision of food for the world was a graphic picture of the way in which he was holding up the name and glory of the LORD to the whole world.

4. Benjamin Trapped by a Trick

How was the rest of the family getting on back in the Promised Land? They had run out of food just like everybody else. They weren't offering any guidance or blessing to the nations. They joined in the crowds going down to Egypt. They bowed down before Joseph just as his dreams had predicted.

Joseph decided to give them a hard time and put them in prison for three days charged with spying. After three days he let them go, but he gave them their money back in their sacks of grain. Jacob and his sons were terrified by this act of grace and kindness (42:35). Joseph had demanded that Benjamin be brought back to Egypt, but Jacob couldn't face the possible loss of his youngest son.

Eventually the famine became too severe and after much pleading and promising, Jacob allows Benjamin to be taken to Egypt. In chapter 43 Jacob is called Israel – he is realising more and more how his schemes are worth nothing. He must simply trust in Christ to care for him and his family.

When Joseph saw Benjamin he was so overcome with emotion that he had to retire to a private room to weep. Nevertheless, he continued to humble his brothers. He hid a divination cup in Benjamin's sack so that they could all be arrested and dragged back to Joseph. They were deeply disturbed and when they thought that Benjamin would be taken, Judah (who had been so arrogant and hypocritical in chapter 38) had to humbly beg for mercy.

Finally, Joseph couldn't contain himself and he let them know who he was. He explained all that the LORD God had done through him over these years. It was clear that Joseph was showing the way forward for the family. He had shown them how to live in gospel faithfulness among pagan people, how to lift up the name of the LORD among the nations.

The whole family came to live in Egypt, away from the Promised Land. God reassured Jacob in a vision (46:1–4). They did not need to fear because the Angel of the LORD said 'I will go down to Egypt with you, and I will surely bring you back again.' Jacob must have been encouraged when he saw how faithful Joseph had become in Egypt. So, they all left the Promised Land to live in the land of Goshen in Egypt.

Chapter 47:7–10 is a striking moment when Jacob actually began to fulfil his evangelistic mission in blessing the nations. The covenant people prospered in this pagan land, although Jacob never forgot the Promised Land (47:29–30).

Further Questions:

1. How did Joseph remain so faithful while he was stuck in prison for so long? Surely he must have felt that his whole life was being wasted?
2. Should Joseph have shared his dreams with his family?
3. Does the Holy Spirit still speak to people with dreams? Do we think He will make it clear whether a dream is from Him or just an ordinary dream?

Genesis 38:1-30

Genesis 38 is perhaps the least popular chapter in the book of Genesis because it is so full of sin, injustice and hypocrisy. Nevertheless, it is precisely for those reasons that it is worth our careful study.

Verses 1-5: Why did Judah separate from his brothers 'at that time'? In light of what the LORD had already said about who to marry, what is so surprising about Judah's choice of wife?

Verses 6-10: Bearing in mind the fact that Jacob's sons are the LORD's chosen family, what is at stake as Judah's wicked sons are judged and condemned by the LORD? Why is Onan's sin so wicked in the LORD's sight?

Verses 11-12: What was Judah's main concern as he postpones giving his son Shelah to Tamar? In light of what Judah had said to Onan (verse 8) why is his action in these verses so wrong?

Verses 13-19: Why was Tamar so interested in being given Shelah as a husband? What was she looking for from Judah's heir?

Verses 20-26: By this stage in the story, we see the downward spiral of wickedness plunging even further and still no sign of Judah turning to the LORD. What seems to be Judah's main concern in these verses? In what ways is Judah seen to be a hypocrite in these verses?

Verses 27-30: How can we see the LORD at work at the end of this episode? Read Ruth 4:18-22 and Luke 3:23-38. What should we learn about the way the LORD works His plans in and through His people?

Week of Readings

Sunday:	Genesis 46 and 47
Monday:	Genesis 37
Tuesday:	Genesis 38
Wednesday:	Genesis 39
Thursday:	Genesis 40 and 41
Friday:	Genesis 42 and 43
Saturday:	Genesis 44 and 45

10. The End of the Beginning

Chapters 48-50

Key Truth: The Israelites end up away from the Promised Land in a pagan nation – but God intended it all for good.

1. Israel Worshipped the LORD

The last verse of chapter 47 is an important verse. Hebrews chapter 11 shows how all the great characters of the Old Testament were examples of faith in Christ. Jacob, in Hebrews 11:21, is striking in that he is only really a 'gospel man' at the very end of his life. 'By faith Jacob, when he was dying, blessed each of Joseph's sons, and worshipped as he leaned on the top of his staff.'

Jacob's words in chapters 48 and 49 of Genesis are full of truth and wisdom. He had spent his life resisting the gospel-covenant, fighting against Christ, but as he finally and fully yielded in his life-long wrestling, he saw reality with such profound clarity.

When Joseph comes to see his dying father, Jacob summarises the covenant blessing in an amazing way: 'God Almighty appeared to me at Luz in the land of Canaan, and there He blessed me and said to me, "I am going to make you fruitful and will increase your numbers. I will make you a community of peoples, and I will give this land as an everlasting possession to your descendants after you."'

At this point Jacob saw that 'Israel' was much bigger than a mere dysfunctional family. Israel is a collection of people from all nations who trust in the LORD, the Promised Seed. Israel is a community of the nations, uniting what sin had divided.

When Jacob blesses Joseph's two sons there is a touch of humour in 48:10 when he can't see the two boys. He must have remembered how he had deceived his father Isaac in just such circumstances. However, Jacob's words of blessing show such faith as he reflected back on his life. They summarise the Christ-centred faith of the believers in Genesis:

May the God before whom my fathers Abraham and Isaac walked, the God who has been my shepherd all my life to this day, the Angel who has delivered me from all harm - may He bless these boys. May they be called by my name and the names of my fathers Abraham and Isaac, and may they increase greatly upon the earth.

Jacob realised that the whole course of his life has been governed by his Shepherd, the Angel of the LORD who had cared for him and blessed him all along. Jacob knows that his own schemes and deceit have been nothing but pointless harm. Everything that he had was a sheer gift of grace from Christ, the God before whom Abraham and Isaac walked.

2. Israel Blessed his Sons

Chapter 49 is Jacob at his best. He is now Israel. He is the man of clear faith. He is full of the Spirit who gives him prophetic insight into the future. This is the man Jacob should always have been. He should always have been Israel, the man who trusted in Christ rather than self, the model of faith for the nations of the world.

Israel spoke to each of his sons, speaking God's Word over each. To each son their deep truth is spoken. To understand and get to the bottom of each of these prophetic declarations we need to follow the life of the tribes named after these sons through the Old Testament.

Reuben's sin of Genesis 35:22 was brought into the open. This tribe amounts to nothing; no significant people ever come out of this tribe.

Simeon and Levi's violence of chapter 34 is finally judged. Their violent character would plague their descendants. They struggle with their hot blood in different ways. Levi tames the hot blood and they give themselves in service to the LORD (Exodus 32:27–29). We are never victims of our own character.

We would expect **Judah** to receive condemnation for the mess of chapter 38, but instead Jacob looks beyond the individual into the future. He saw that king David and his descendants would be of the tribe of Judah, and that they would hold that power until the Promised Seed, the Messiah Himself would also be born of this tribe (verse 10). The blessing to the nations of the covenant people depends upon and is achieved by Christ. This prophecy sets out what had been told to Abraham long ago, but now it is Judah who is specified as being the ancestor of the Christ.

Jacob saw beyond the initial settlement in the Promised Land at the time of Joshua to a time when the tribe of **Zebulun** would occupy the coast.

The tribe of **Issachar** would have a tough burden to carry – but the quality of their land would make up for it.

Dan would provide justice for Israel – perhaps this comes through Samson in Judges 12–16.

Here there is an interlude (verse 18) as Jacob is very close to death. He blurts out the great truth that is close to his heart – that he is waiting for the salvation of the LORD. He speaks of Christ, the Promise he had spoken of in 49:10. Then the blessings resume.

Gad would be good at fighting for Israel, see 1 Chronicles 12. (The men of Gad make up David's mighty men.)

Asher is noted for great wealth and luxuries. (In Joshua 19, they have some of Israel's great trading places.)

Naphtali means 'struggle'. He is set free from this for peace and friendship, rather than war.

Israel's favourite sons are left to last.

Joseph's blessing is a huge tribute to the sovereign goodness of the Rock of Israel – it's all about what the LORD has done. Joseph could never have engineered his own success. A few times he was as good as dead, but the LORD had His eye on him. Life does not depend on our own ingenuity but upon the blessings of the LORD.

It is surprising that **Benjamin** is called a 'ravenous wolf'. He seemed quite a quiet and peaceful chap earlier on when we met him. But Jacob is able to see the future. In Judges 20 and 21, the Benjamites go to war against all the rest of Israel. The Apostle Paul was also a Benjamite. He showed wicked violence in his early life then tremendous passion and zeal after he became a Christian.

Who would have thought this mix of characters had any kind of future at all? It is only because of the Promised Messiah that they are given a promising future.

The great speech that Israel has just given to his sons is one of the most amazing and specific prophetic utterances in the whole Bible. Even a man called 'Deceit' is not a victim of his own nature because of the promises of the LORD. He had lived by his own nature for so long yet now he abandons himself to his LORD.

4. Israel Died in Egypt

Israel's death is a faithful death. He knows where he is going. He will be gathered to his people in paradise. He is going to Abraham, Sarah, Isaac, Rebekah. Even as he is dying, he still thinks about his people, the nation of Israel. He gives very specific instructions about where he is to be buried. After 17 years of living in Egypt, he ensures his descendants would not forget their inheritance, their true hope – even though they were to spend 400 years in exile in pilgrimage in Egypt. Jacob is turned into an Egyptian mummy (50:3). This takes a long time and it was probably necessary for his body to be transported. Tremendous respect is shown by the Egyptians for Jacob's household. In chapters 42–45, Jacob had been so worried about dying without his sons around him. But he dies with them all and they all carry his body back with respect and grief.

It is worth noting that when this Pharaoh is asked 'Let us go', he immediately says 'go!' and even offers help with going. 400 years later, in the book of Exodus, that is not what the Pharaoh would say.

Joseph's brothers have tortured consciences, and rightly so. They cannot forget how they treated Joseph when they sold him as a slave. They make up an outrageous story – it is no wonder that Joseph wept when he heard their message. They think they need to atone for their wrongs by putting themselves into slavery. But Joseph has come to understand the great truth of the universe. The LORD God is on the throne. It's not for Joseph to pass judgement on his brothers. The gospel of Jesus Christ had removed all bitterness from Joseph's heart. He is happy to forgive his brothers. Even though (verse 20), they had originally meant it for evil, God had infinitely better plans. We are not able to overthrow God's purposes, even through our evil deeds. We remember back in Genesis chapter 3 that even as Adam and Eve were judged for their sin, the gospel was preached. Even as the LORD brings terrible judgement through the flood, the gospel is proclaimed through the building of the Ark.

Throughout the book of Genesis, we see the LORD had His eye on the good things accomplished at the end. Those who trust the gospel of the living God are caught up into these promises and enjoy them as a free gift. Even in opposing them, people are forced to serve God's purposes. There's no point in us opposing Him; we cannot resist Him. He always accomplishes His purposes, just as He said He would. The whole creation belongs to the God who is Father Son and Holy Spirit. In Acts 2:23, even wicked intentions are used to accomplish the Cross of Jesus, where the glory of God shines its very brightest. He works all things for the good of those who love Him, Romans 8:28.

But what an ending to this great story! Joseph dies and is buried. There is nothing more for 400 years. No glorious return to the Promised Land. Joseph becomes a mummy. The book of Genesis would seem to begin in a deathless universe and end in a coffin. However, after we have learnt of the sovereign rule of the Living God and how He accomplishes His plans, we are filled with expectation instead. This is not a weak ending for the faithful reader. It's a page-turner.

Further Questions:

1. Like those brothers, most of us have aspects of our personalities that will always challenge our Christian discipleship. What is the Bible's lesson for us as we face these problems?
2. When we see 'great evil' in the world, we might think it is undermining the purposes of God. How does Joseph's life give us a new perspective on tragedy and disaster?
3. Hebrews 11:21 draws attention to the fact that Jacob leaned on his staff as he blessed his sons. Can we think of other significant ways that staffs are used in the Bible?

Genesis 50: 15-21

This seems like a strange way to end the first book of the Bible. But when we read this story, we see there are many important truths for life that we learn from this fascinating chapter.

Verses 15–17: Why did Joseph's brothers even think up this plan? How must they have been feeling all these years since chapter 37?

Verse 17: Why do you think Joseph wept when he heard what his brothers had said? (Look also at Genesis 45:4–9)

Verse 18: Were Joseph's brothers doing the right thing by apologising and offering to make it up to him? What does it show about their view of forgiveness?

Verses 20–21: The brothers did a terrible thing to Joseph. How was it possible for Joseph to forgive and show kindness to them?

Do we sometimes feel God could not possibly forgive us for something we've done? Or perhaps we are holding a grudge and refusing to forgive someone. What is the godly response to these things, shown by Joseph in this passage? Think also of Jesus' teaching on forgiveness, e.g. Matthew 18:25–35 and Luke 7:36–50.

Verse 20: How can a correct understanding of the Father's providence help us to trust Him in our everyday life?

Week of Readings

Sunday:	Revelations 21:10–27
Monday:	Genesis 48
Tuesday:	Genesis 49
Wednesday:	Genesis 50
Thursday:	Exodus 1
Friday:	Exodus 13:19 and Joshua 24:32 and Hebrews 11:22
Saturday:	Deuteronomy 33

3